Swans

New Poems (1890-1891)

With, in appendix, chapter one, book two, of *Francis Vielé-Griffin: His Work, His Thought, His Art* by Jean de Cours.

Francis Vielé-Griffin

Translated By Richard Robinson

Sunny Lou Publishing Company
Portland, Oregon, USA
http://www.sunnyloupublishing.com

1st Edition, Revised and Corrected: December 28, 2025
Original Publication Date: July 7, 2022

ISBN: 978-1-955392-30-3

# # #

This translation from French is based on the
Léon Vanier, Libraire-Éditeur edition of
Les Cygnes, Paris, 1892.

The translation, in appendix, is from chapter one,
book two, of *Francis Vielé-Griffin: Son Oeuvre,
Son Pensée, Son Art,* by Jean de Cours,
published by the Librairie Ancienne Honoré
Champion, Paris, 1930.

Contents

Swans

Do you remember...

Do you remember yesterday with smiles
On its face, tears on its cheeks,
And all the matutinal rosinesses?
Then, braiding flowers, which you tied into garlands,
We sang our triumphal aubades;
Then, toward the empyrean, its vertigoes braved,
We followed, toward the future, with eyes raised,
The brilliant flight of swans!...

Here are, this evening, the vineyards
Heavy with tomorrows' harvest:
While extending our hand
– Your white hands are worthy,
Your hands shall be my hands –
We cull, here and there, such bunches that
A single stock promises a quarter muid
And a whole month's wine weighs on the lintel;
And the shadow of the old porch, dear to swallows,
Is made of the inebriety of new hours;
And the vineyard grows from coteau to coteau...

Lying at your feet, I dreamt this afternoon:
We walked among the stalks, across the reaped meadow,
It was night, and above us, near the stars,
Passed a wedge of swans with white sails.
And the one with silk moiré ribboned
Around its neck, that no sun could wither;
And that one bore a diadem
Vainly promised for the sweetest poem;
The other held the flower that never fades,
That no one harvests;
They passed northward, majestic and calm,
Glorious with an echo in their pinions

– Of a slow rhythm of oars,
Of an evening breeze among the palms,
Of ancient voices.

We followed them to a poplar near,
Importunate chatter of a thousand voices...

One of them, spreading its wings against the night
– A flower fully bloomed, filled with pain –
Appeared crucified,
Its wings trembling from the supreme disaster
In a cry of deified desire,
And it was a star!

Here is the moiré that nothing fades,
That floated, that I seized in flight;
And here is my diaphanous heart
To make you a bright pent-à-col with.

The other came falling, spiraling
Among the tall, bowed lilies;
And I wept upon seeing it
As one weeps to see hopes dashed;
The diadem came to crown
A sleep encrimsoned with roses;
I took it from amongst the thorns
To give to you – Sweet head! –
For you were fairer than all else to me:
And here it is, the diadem
That no poet merited,
O you, the sweetest of poems.

But the other – with the opened flower
That was floating before it –
Sang above us until dawn broke
The song that everyone hears in their dreams
Night after night,

And when the sun rose from the sea, toward the strand,
The swan, opening wide its wings to the vermilion kiss,
Was swallowed up, with the flower, into the sun...

Here I am, eyes lowered, walking and dreaming and loving you;
The unspoilt moiré is yours by right of love
And the crown is still yours, for maint days;
But the Flower of Forbidden Joy – it is supreme,

And it is of this that these poems speak.

The Stopping Place

Je suis bon à tous. – JULES LAFORGUE

Stop,
Hear me, my brother, who pass;
Be quiet:
I know our soul, tender and tired,
When you were walking without looking, nor seeing,
In the direction of some hope
Ancient and dear – or young, barely loved,
Like a half-heard laugh that one follows, mocking,
Or like a long-lost look that one goes searching after,
Walking,
Walking – from October to May;
I know your heart, my heart.

Look; think with my chosen words;
Despite the heavy flux of your blood,
That beats against your temple, wave after wave,
Dream in my chosen words:
With your gay whistling through the broom
And all the golden, blinding sunlight
– So that you were walking, eyes half-closed
On the path that led you –
You were joyful merely for some hope?

Is it about Her? With a kiss to gather?
I know your heart – you cannot be merry otherwise;
Toward Her kiss, which knows how to age,
Walk, then, drunk through the young hay:
You cannot be drunk otherwise.

If it is not about Her – sit; you are sad:

Beside her, there are no other joys;
Life is serious and death is sinister:
With its wings spread in enormous flight,
Its shadow on life is of a bird of prey.

Certainly, you will not have despaired:
Wrapping your will around you
– As one wraps a coat drenched with rain –
You walk straight,
You know you are immortal and you defy
Time which you know to be illusory.
But you fear dying, for one hour even
– One hour!... you see it well, the hour grips you,
My human brother.

You are sad;
Every memory is a tomb without Christ,
The road that has led you here
From an old concern toward a young concern
– If you turned around, hand to brow,
Like someone who looks far away,
As do,
At the gates of tombs, tall marble watchmen –
The road is lined with crosses
And from tree to tree...
Your beautiful love, your young idea!

So that your laughter turns into a sob
And your cherished hope becomes unbearable.

O! Believe me! [You] who think on the morrow:
Excessive joy is sorrowful and so much so
That the soul, in its grief, exults immortal,
To weep is sweet above all else;
Sit down beside me;
When I wept, head in hand,
I saw, between my fingers, that slow grey light turn pink:

At that time, my soul had faith.

And you, my sister, who pass,
I know you are sad too, despite what you do;
Though you dress your disquiet in gaiety,
Though you trail over the gravel, fleur-de-lys'd,
The haughty hem of your dress of a prude,
Or, though your lips be full with kisses
That your hand takes and casts – like a poor woman
Who, thinking herself rich, empties her begging bowl
By the handsful for other beggars;
Your soul is in distress,
Daughter of man.

Beyond your small, pretty fever,
At the mercy of desire, your mirror,
What do you know of your grace? If, indeed, it is?
Sadness made you a sign each evening,
Showing life as well, and what it was worth,
So that your poor lip trembles a little
And your long gaze grows dim.

Sit down, my sister, and weep:
To weep is beautiful above all else;
It is only one hour, but it lasts
Eternal in metamorphoses:
The hour of holy pity and superhuman love
That weeps until it smiles... at last.

The Ford

Un étrange suicide. Une jeune fille, s'etant vêtue de blanc, s'est avancée délibérément dans la mer, où elle s'est noyée. Son corps a eté rejeté par les vagues. – FAITS DIVERS[1]

"Over there;
Every dream lives on eternity,
Every winged thought sings in the branches
In the springtime,
Over there;
One hour, always the same, clear or slow
Of the same new joy in its gaiety,
Of a love one does not weep for,
Of the white kisses of idylls
Fallen from the wings of smiling archangels;
They are islands,

Over there,
With the flowering trees in bloom
In the springtime;
The Saints whom the bad have killed;
And God, who passes, calling his virgins
Toward the softly radiant parvis
Where the stars are candles
In the lace of the clouds...

She is in the springtime
Over there,
My mother – and the other sister whom I did not know –
Who cull bouquets of white lilies,
– As we did – in the clear evening –
Last spring –

---

[1]*Un étrange... vagues*: French for "A strange suicide. A girl, dressed in white, deliberately walked into the sea, where she drowned herself. Her body was washed back by the waves." – Divers Facts

And watching for my arrival
While looking at the sea;

For Christ told me it is good to die,
That fine sunny morning
When he came to me in his winged ciborium
Consoling me with love, and healing me:
I saw him beaming near my lips
In a kiss of engagement,
Beyond the choir and the walls
And in my revealed body
I heard him clearly calling me.

At night, I prayed until the white of dawn;
And when, raising my head,
I saw the casement grow pale,
All my hope was in celebration
And, in my daring soul
Filled with impatient love,
I thought: It is, perhaps, Him
Who comes, who shines,
Here is my turn, here is the escort!...
I listened, eyes closed, until full morning;
Hardly believing He could have left me there in his kindness,
That I had not died
And been taken in his kiss of eternity.

Day came, came again, always the same;
And the other woman with her hard soul,
With her haughty expression,
(So sweetly smiling at my perjured father)
Who said, in passing: The lunatic!

And when I wept because of it, far away, in the garden
– Where we had culled the white lilies
Last spring
While looking at the sea

So blue and clear
In the morning light –
Thinking of all that is no longer,
Of all that will be, over there,
I was sought out with intrusive cries
– My disquieted father and the other who feigned; –
My heart was bleeding
And I did not respond to them.

At that time, there were parties and balls,
Flowers that one throws, carnivals,
Countless evenings
With the role that one must play;
One evening, in the park, where I was weeping in the shade
For all that,
The vile kiss came and brushed my cheek;
And the surprise and their loud laughter,
The promise and the betrothals
And their gala.
Bad days and worse evenings;
The flesh with its reprisals;
All that love that one lauds and vaunts,
All that love that frightens me
Comes murmuring, at evening, with strange words
That make me weep and wring my hands and which I have fled,
All that love of skillful expression.
And the mystery of its night
And of its words...

Behold the wedding day
– Is that not the bell tolling
As on Sundays? –
All of yesterday I was gay – they said, wise;
I picked lilacs with white roses
Until the bright crepuscule

While looking at the sea;
Everyone was laughing, even the other was good to me.
– Is not that the bell tolling?...
My father spoke to me, tender almost, I believe:
You are going to go away, he said, far away from us,
To live happily ever after with the husband of your choice
– And I responded to him all joyous:
I will leave tomorrow with the Spouse.

Behold the nuptial day!
Here is my white dress and my immaculate soul,
Here is the end of all my strife
Of which I am tired, when I was cowardly;
Here are your white lilacs, mother, and your white roses,
And here is the pale light of dawn,
– Calm like a Sunday –
Here is the dawn,
And here is the sea, blue and calm,
Which leads to God...

Look, one gives the signal?...
My mother of mine, waits for me over there
To give to my Spouse my unworthy soul,
My love, weary
From prayer,
My desire tired,
My heart of little...
Oh! Here I come, mother,
And you, Sweet Lord God,
Behold the ford..."

She walks toward the sea.

On the Sill

*Au seuil du monde, où – comme Ulysse Polytlas, aux confins du Gades
extrème de son voyage, le regard perdu aux lointains crépusculaires du
désert d'au-delà – tout homme voit l'ombre de sa mere, pale, vaine...*
– CARLYLE.

From this hour, to that one, there is but –
There is but one poor instant – only one! – the last-born;
Maybe, by fixing my blindness
On the night that falls or the day that breaks,
(As from a boat one sees the coast appear in the distance)
I will see Eternity coming...

It is good to live the poor life,
The gorgeous blue river where the heart veers off course;
It is good to walk through meadows
When the road retaken would have been twice as tiring;
I see that it is good to live the good life;
It is like a love whose flame is low,
That dies, and one laughs at it – but weeps later.

I think also that the sun was such
Over the course of that vain day, gentle and mortal,
For the duration of those Junes, by the meadows and banks,
By the bright hillsides, by the misty valley
(Red, and pink with poppies, and pale blue, and golden!)
That there is no more gorgeous glory for my eyes,
That there is no gentler light unnoticed
– And the voice of the leaves and the voices within them,
I do not know of a more beautiful music.

A regret comes from all that;
Could one not have lived according to Life?
Could one not, according to other laws,
(Which it knows, doubtless, and which it would have told us about,

If only we had faith),
Have loved it *another way* and according to its heart
And according to the secret of its sound
Of laughter, of loves, of maternity,
And have been loved in return, the entire summer,
And have lived on its immortality?...

I was taken from it, by words
Sounding false in the dawn – I remember:
The tall green wheat, the new wheat
– A childhood forest – and their cornflowers;
I know of no sweeter dream than my own:
The warm and soft road for bare feet,
The surprised brotherly blackbird,
And the big clear sky above the ears of wheat,
The spring wherein I saw myself with wonder
– They made a sin of it, of my universe,
Before the open book.

There it is, open, still, and I have made it,
Gentler than all those ever read of, dreamt of,
More dolorous and sacred, more chaste and tender
Than their songs of trouvères,
Than their most beautiful, wondrous poem:
With my heart, with my soul, with my flesh,
With my eyes,
I have made my beautiful book of life – ardent and bright...

To die? I have no fear of the darkness
– The soft darkness that follows
Beneath the moonlight,
Beneath the big, radiant sun;
Often, as a child, I have closed both eyes
To see the night;
And when, weeping for love (one weeps for love),

I desired to die by its kiss,
It was my joy, and it was with all its heart;
– This evening, I am afraid...
No, it is like a regret, rather;
We have died a hundred times – yesterday, this afternoon –
With our hours of all ages
And this one here, is it strange?
Will we not say, *tomorrow*, this evening?
And like yesterday – and with more hope?
Have we not died a hundred times:
Where is the child dreamer we were told about?
Where all our evenings? our kisses, our desires for Her?
– Ah! really, all is vain, death is beautiful!...

If I had lived... but let us leave these things;
Maybe by fixing my eyes on this night
(Or toward that day which makes my eyelids pink),
Maybe by closing my eyes *to see the night*
I shall be able to see Eternity coming...

Here it is!
I see... I see the past, O so pale,
So distant – am I dead to see it like this? –
I see, as if through a basement window:
The dark blue sky
And along the gray road
A shadow...
No! Now everything iridesces:
The horizon turns; a lake emerges from the mist;
Dawn! Daybreak, the triumphant morning,
And the breeze chattering in a childlike voice...

Do you see?...
See how prodigious the sun is:
There is not a blade of grass it has not adorned;
Let me see; what time is it?
– What is it that makes you tired, my heart:

The great gentle day unfurls!
My heart, my heart, my heart, your beautiful April!
My heart, your joy!...

I am as if stunned, the horizon veers
Along the zigzags of a path beneath the firs
That weep – it was in this way, those long mornings,
When I watched for the word they wanted to say –
And, beyond the old glacier,
There is the path –
I was one with all that, those things and I,
We smiled long days together...

The plains;
The voices among the aspens;
The oak grove;
The stubble, the flocks, the river;
The blue shadow and the new grass;
– Let me sleep in this shade,
I am very weary – the wind clamors in the reeds;
Why deny me everything?
And why lead me like a child...

This way?
Still the gray road, the dark blue sky;
The day dies, ah! Here is a shadow passing,
It's yours, Mother... Mama!
I am very weary;
Why the night, why the end, why
This mad love within me
For your smile, young, there in the distance,
Pale, vain, in my memory of your summer
– Which passes, far away from me... Like eternity...

The Swineherd

Here, among the oaks,
The shade is a strange mirror
Of reveries
And all the flowers are such as live
Old lives,
Pensively;
And when I muse, while gazing at the plains
That roll beyond the branches, low as a fringe,
In the distance,
The forgotten hours pass like corteges
– Or almost – for here I am an old man:
They pass
Towards the sun-bathed hills
As if singing,
Like girls and stripling youth,
And I close my eyes;
From here, among the trunks
Verdant with strangely soft moss;
Standing, I follow the merry play of rays
Falling on the black backs of my swine
Grubbing in the earth, among the fallen leaves,
In such ways
That, often,
I must smile, I think,
Recalling that I was another in the past.

Before the evening when I went off along the paths
– My heart beating louder than the bay mare's gallop –
My father was harsh and craven and bent
Under the young yoke made by the hands
Of the other whom he took when my mother died:
I played my part slamming the door behind me
And galloped off into the night towards Life, and the door
Resounded with its slam in my heart that beat
Like the gallop of an escort.

Voices,
Too,
Come to me from over there,
Or pass by, whispering, among the leaves:
In the old days,
We had wandered throughout the night
From sills to shelves,
I, the sower of gold, and they here,
Couples of joy and noise,
Toward the jubilation of the leaves;
Alone, I was alone, although at my arms
Weighed – barely – a laugh of tenderness
And their gown rustled at my knees:
Weary, we came to the edge of the wood at dawn:
Behind us, the town emerges from the fog
And unfolds in golden domes
And rises
In fiery minarets
Or falls, from terrace to terrace,
Down to the sea – white town in its charm –
And, before me, the mysterious awakening of darkness
– Where I walked for days on end,
Wherein my virgin soul was wrapped,
Where my heart sleeps.

It seems like only yesterday that I left them
With their laughter and the inebriation of all flesh.
And the full awakening of the domes and their gaieties
And all the argentine ripples of the seas...

Sometimes, in the spring, when the eglantine snows
And I fear treding on some lovers
In the new grass
And when I hear the neighing
Of mares on the road where the dust
Flows before the rain,

I think I can still hear them coming
Watching, between the branches, their cortege
And I prepare to tell them everything, too
– Joyful to tell them everything, like this:
My life and all the calmness in my soul
Living among the oaks and the scent of sap
And the peaceful animals
And all the forest that sings and troats;
And my heart beats and searches for old phrases
That I made sing according to my dream,
I repeat them softly,
But – searching my memory –
I'm afraid they will not understand,
So I fear to see them return.

There, near the eglantine,
Between those last oaks,
Arching over the path
That descends, from above, along the opposite hillside
(So that from here it seems to ascend to the sky
And its coming brightness)
It was Lise the devout,
At times,
And Marc the handsome;
– They wore the same silk;
All day long one laughed at their quarrel,
Which ended in that long-awaited kiss
At the hour of joy;
I found her less beautiful
Than before, and he seemed more foolish
– But what do they matter?

At other times, along the oak grove's edge,
It is Laure who walks, along the border, in the grass
– She loved that –
With a spray of flowers,
And her golden hair,

Here, there;
Her lips were closed to every bee,
Despite Euphorion's sad gaiety,
But always such that he marvels at her.
And we all laughed
– And I wake up...

Everything is bizarre here, for a long time now;
I dream while hearing things,
Many an unknown thing;
Oftentimes I have laughed at a dream that seized me
Like a bird caught in a snare,
And at the things one says with lips closed,
That one recounts to oneself alone, musing...

One day as I was gathering chestnuts,
Tossing them, one by one, into the sack (for I count them,
In my head, before tying it)
They passed, laughing, near me,
On the sunken path of the valley,
Ribbons floating yellow and pink,
And two on each horse,
With their voices so sudden
That I started, as if with shame,
And lay down in the brush,
Speechless,
Holding my breath,
As if I had been stealing
The chestnuts.

And then, when I called to them,
They had already passed.

Flavie.
I saw her again one evening,

Near the spring where I go to drink in the evening,
For many long old days of life now,
Leading my pigs;
She was bent to drink from her cupped hand;
I did not dared to speak to her, thinking of the days gone by;
But when I said to her: "Flavie!"
Speaking of the other life,
Of Marc and Lise and the group,
Of what they would say if they saw me here
With my swine and my clothes
And my spear for every weapon,
She looked at me so sadly
That I felt warm tears in my eyes:
"You poor dear," she said and departed.

Often, I have thought for an entire night about that scene.

And when, yonder, in the pale crepuscule,
The extreme horizon darkens,
– Like an iron taken from the fire, going from red to blue of night, –
I love to say,
With eyes closed: "Today is the day!"
Turning towards some old scrap of life gone by;
But I no longer have a memory:
Every dream I have comes alive and speaks
To the point where it is always a future
And I go on recalling to myself
What should have been
– I, gentler, and Flavie,
Less vain and less amorous,
Euphorion and Marc, more manly
And Lise, just as she is, and Laure, the same, maybe...
And I name them...

However, I should have liked to tell them,

That nothing is sad in the shade of my oaks,
That everything, outside the forest, is worse;
That I am not alone, seeing eyes,
Amongst the leaves where her train rustles,
Flavie, or whomever I wish,
Without reproach;
And for having placed my head amidst the mosses
And gazed up at the azure that seems near
Between the pink branches of young shoots,
– Two cold stones in my feverish fists –
I can tell them, knowing how to intoxicate them with it,
That all the sweetness of their kisses
Blossoms and sings here better than on their lips.

I will tell them
That nothing weeps here,
And that the autumn wind, too,
Which some think is sad, is a hymn of hope;
I will tell them
That nothing is sad here, morning or evening,
Except, in the distance,
When November rustles in the branches
Driving the leaves down white paths
– They skirt away, it chases them back
Until they drop, exhausted,
Then it passes and laughs –
That nothing is sad here,
Except, in the distance, on the opposite hillside,
Monotonous like a [bell] chiming same note,
The shock of axes brandished all day,
Heavy and muted.

I should have liked to tell them
That all sadness lies in the sad gaze
Of their eyes which cannot read
This book here, where all Words persist
Mutable and the same and so that one can die
In a dream and believe one grows green again

And rise like an oak (just as one saw
Those elders of yesteryear do – so it is said –)...
And he who knows how to read
Your open page,
Green forest!
Smiles in the end...

I would like to tell them
That I am not a fool.

Eurythmy

"Your poised hand is like a fruit on this branch,
As for a bright fruit, I am thirsty for your pale hand;
The shadowy forest is fragrant and the night grows frightened
In the month of blossoming lilies and offered lips,
– O smile poised among the green leaves! –
Queen, I am hungry for a kiss from your mouth...

For your breath lightly grazes and passes
In such a dawn of adolescent soul
That, for a lifetime, it wanders never weary
Towards the hope of the kiss that your pity may grant,
Hebe of the pain poured out in balm,
Imperial love of souls who wander alone,
O bright veil, weft of darkness, where the woof shines,
Shuddering swan's wingspan,
O you who in the folds of your veil enshroud
The fiancé of joy elected by an exceptional fate..."

"Here you are, as on the evening of your first ecstasy,
Sad with the wine of my beauty;
I have given you all the gold of the legacy,
All the gold jealous of your expression,
And here you are, weeping to me of your poverty;
Life has flowed like a river, for seven years,
And you carry me along, as in the parable.
The treasures of lights that I had given you
Still heavy with the earth where you buried them
So that your weak eyes were not blinded
By the symbol's beams;
I have dressed you in hope and crowned you with summer,
[You] who come trailing your nakedness towards me,
All your heart obscured by sensual doubt;
On the eagle before you, my word of joy
Burned in the ritual, but you have not sung!

See: to your extended thirst, as into a cup,
I have poured all the wine of maturing auroras;
I have made grow on you, that forever you might pray,
The majesty of voices in a murmuring vault;
I have sown the parvis with the playthings of my smile,
I have draped the pillars with vine-leaf volutes
And stretched from arch to arch a soft flight of choirs;
I have pierced the forest of worked trellis
With the gleam from my azured rosaces
Whence fall the rays of my lyre into your hands;

The temple is such that every shiver converges and sings
Around the altar where I have laid your soul before you,
And in such a way that all the love of the living earth
Might vibrate, in your voice even, to sing to me finally;

If over you the heavy shadow thickens its darkness,
Sob elsewhere over your excruciating fears;
If doubt, making thirsty your insatiate thirsts,
Fills your empty cup with the illusions of opprobrium,
What more can I do for you? Walk: you have set yourself free;
Turn elsewhere your lament which insults me,
Your alone desire for the vow of my worship lightens your load;
Leave the temple in mourning for a sacrilege;
Towards the phantom that you dream of following
Go, you are free: rejoice...

At the crossroads of doubt,
Choose; here is the road:
Take hatred and pride in your hands
– The Sword and the Buckler –
Go fashioning your tomorrows
From the hour when – behold: you are your own master,
And be whoever you wish to be;
Leave in the direction of pitched battle,
Attempt insult and, having attempted, kill:
Insult is sweet when one has avenged it

And the day only repays you for what it has cost;
In the evening it will do good to have lived
Life epic after epic;
Go, take your pride, your buckler,
And take your hatred, your sword;
Leave for the Life where victory smiles
On the valiant one whose glaive has dispelled the dream;
Speak up: only a cry is heard;
Stand tall, that your shadow may lengthen!..."

"O madness evoked in glories!
Fanfares sound in the hollow valley of battles!
The organ weeps with expiatory hymns in the night;
And the people acclaim from atop the walls
The vanquisher fanned by the wing of victories.

A sailor sings
An overseas dirge;
A herdsman repeats to himself the name of the conquerer;
– It rains; the wind blows –
Far off, in the bright crepuscule,
An errant knight rides in the vale.

Voices mingle in the darkness
Without response to the distances of memories;
The sound of countless steps is lost
In the cathedrals of histories;
The choir grilles creak in the shadow;
The past retracts its black wings...

Is this the dream of your glories?..."

"Here is your path: walk
Where the trail takes you, as the path leads you,
Leave or gather the eglantine's flame

According as the breeze inclines it;
And according to the words of those who go –
Speak, pray, and chant along the way;
To others repeat what others will say;
Let those who will run run
And those who will tarry tarry;
Press forward at neither a slow nor a rapid pace;
And may God provide for tomorrow..."

"A flock returns in the twilight;
Voices, dear and banal, fill the air;
Smoke from thatched roofs rises in spirals;
A blessed peace circulates in the night;
– And formal dress is the dress of mourning;
Naïve hope and credulous faith –
In the penumbra with vesperal pallors
One chants, on the step of the thresholds...
Is it the chant of your fatal nights?
Is it the peace of your pride?..."

"Come here, come,
Outside the act, far from the dream;
Die, this very evening, your brief hour;
Do not project, do not remember;
– Life is strange and crazy,
Future or present or past –
Stifle your expression in silence,
Spare the sound of your steps
And the vain noise of your thought;
Do not wish, do not dream;
Blind yourself with the immensity;
Resorb, into the All, your vain vanity
And silence your joy so that sorrows may sleep..."

"Spare my wounded soul;
I know the sweet pain of your raillery;
If the old flood of tears ran dry
The rose of laughter would be withered by it
– I have wept only in the shadow of my best evenings –
Life is good in the gentle flowers,
But life is holy in the flowering bramble
That one culls in the harvest of your prairie;
No call summons me to the mud of paths
Nor the dust of cavalcades;
Is there anything in me that you do not sense,
Queen of the unscythed plains?
My only desire is toward your compassionate hands
And toward the shadow lying at your soft feet:

On my bowed soul
– Source of dawn where your laughter shed its petals –
You reflected your image forever,
So that I have kept on my soul
The shadow of your smile, forever,
– Floating shadow of palm –
You who mix joy and pain in your laughter,
Wisdom and folly in your dawn laughter,
You were passing by in a scent of myrrh
And all May shed its petals into the fold of your dress:
'Sing to the echo that laughed in response'
– And you laughed at dawn –
'For nothing is spoken that does not remain to be said.'
– And all May shed its petals into the fold of your dress. –

I loved you with a love of music
On the lute engarlanded with jasmine.
With a love of the faithful and of the priest
Who loses himself in canticles
From yesterday to tomorrow;
And so softly did I call out your name
That from one love another was born,
So that my love and you were but one

And the love song became the beloved;
I have sinned for having too gently called out your name...

Too many vain, dead, verbose songs
Accumulate in our mournful memories:
We have read the road at too many milestones,
Asked the way at too many gates;
I want the rose, o Queen, with which you adorn yourself,
I want the lily, which you hold in your hand.

O you who alone recomfort,
Have I told you of the trying night?
When the wing is weary and drags, hampering the angel,
When the star fell like a meteor
Toward a strange dawn,
When I felt the solitude,
Of living according to you in the aurora-less dawn?
Ah! I would have loved your solitude
When your new dawn was not bound to turn pale...

Queen, I thirst for the pale wine of your certitude!..."

"Soft, strangely soft, in a dawning crepuscule,
Such was the bright star in the branches of the willow grove;
Melodiously soft, as if rising from the valleys,
In an idyllic dawn, a dream of sobs;
As soft as, sounds of lapses and waves,
The night that grows calm far from the seas of tiled shadows,
And so soft that the shock of their mêlées falls silent
And every soul listens, seated, with eyes closed,
– Do you hear the hosanna of unequaled hymns?

Dispersed within you, do you feel tomorrow's aurora,
Blood of glory, flowing in the heart that keeps you alive?
Held out toward you, from the shadow where your hope deviates,
Do you feel the cold pommel of a glaive in your hand?
Time on every road passes like a phantom:

Cast the crooked glaive with its cold pommel far away from you,
And toward the auroral empurplement of the dome
Chant the hymn of love that weeps deep inside you;

That your size, without redress, may dominate them:
Your simple voice will sing some extraordinary song,
For my certitude inclines over you
And my love of love dazzles you!

Nothing but my glory prevails,
Nothing but the shadow of my love gives shelter;
To the ones the vaunted victory,
To the others the dream with its muted silence,
But to the one I love devolves
The poem of Life:
The victor is your gesture and the saint your thought;
For my glory, just as I willed it,
In slow or hurried rhythms,
Evolves and deviates;

To the simple Poem,
As in the forest at dawn,
The rhythm goes round clear and ample
As in the folds of my robe,
As in the circuits of my supple wave;

A voice sounds from yesterdays to tomorrows:
A priest speaks over the indifferent crowd;
A mother smiles wisdom in vain words;
A messenger repeats hurried phrases;
From evenings to mornings,
Clear or muted, never silent,
Vibrant, passed from hand to hand,
The lyre sings,
From poet to poet
– Hymn in the wind of hope towards the sought-after future;

Walks, returns, and pauses –

The choir of metamorphoses
Traces my consummated glories;
And it is the smile of roses
And it is the voice of boughs
And it is the soul of things
That your soul has dearly loved:

In my May orchard – I had told you this –
In my May orchard every rose smiles,
The sun forms pearls of tears on the petals,
A branch swings a song of the nest,
Sweetness emanates from matinal scents;

In my May valley every arum spreads,
The sun is blinded by the moving mirror,
A stream rolls a dream along in its laughter,
A spider spins in the reeds,
A bird gazes at its reflection;

Beneath my May forest every honeysuckle blooms,
The sun in gold beams trickles through the thick shade,
A roebuck makes noises in the leaves that it gathers,
The breeze passes along the row of birches,
From leaf to leaf;

Throughout my May plain, all the grasses sheen silver,
The sun shines there like a fencing match,
A bee buzzes in the muguets along the path
Where the tall flowers cluster near the brook,
The breeze sings along the row of ashes..."

"Queen, your glance is the world itself
It is but one incomparable rose.
The rose of love and of every poem,
The rose that your glance created;

It is but a bee in the golden light of morning,

It is but a bird on the bending branch,
It is but a single, long, childlike dream,
O mother, let me dream in your holy joy;

O intense and prodigious radiance,
Lightning whenas you smile from thing to thing,
Beneath the joyous day of your limpid glory;
It is but a Bee, a Bird, but a Rose!

In the slow, indefinite harmony
– Harmonic chain that dawn draws,
Cords of the Orphic lyre of Life –
Passes and repasses the song of nests
– Weft of joy weaving your dress
From April to April, Eurythmy;

Clothed in ephemeral wonder,
Girt with the song radiant of your grace
That the lilies gild in their chaste embrace
Of ardent powder,
[She] sows in the morning rain all forgetfulness of her vigil,
That the Flower that Sings might bloom and perfume the air.

What wing beats like a heart brimming with joy?
What sowing of lilies rises in clouds?
What perfume, clear like a flight, deploys?
Queen, in what dream have you adorned me?"

  Sounds of the forest

We have hoped, we have hoped.

  Distant voices

The darkness grows heavy
With the weight of incalculable hours;
Impure life has lied about it
And stagnates since the Eden of receded sources

Far into the exasperated future,
– There is no longer an ultimate Thule –

Sounds of the forest

We have hoped for as long as an eternity.

Distant voices

Man stoops with age,
Hateful for no longer being his own god:
And walks trembling in his scant rage,
And with his scant love he plays a game;
Vain, however, for having compared himself to himself
– His pride is small –

Sounds of the forest

We have hoped since time immemorial.

More-distant voices.

Drunkenness is sad and sniggers;
The vision is veiled in a shadow, as well;
The Standard, flower of glory,
Hangs from its shaft and fades;
The Bread, in the leprous ciborium, has molded;
The Wine of the centuries has evaporated
– The night is black –

Sounds of the forest

We have hoped since time immemorial.

At Helen's Grave

Argument

Dead!
Among the blue willows, fainted;
In the mirror of the pond, slain by the breeze;
Did you care nothing for our escort
Of dazzling youth
For You alone striven?

You whose voice repeats the same words
That make love sing for all eternity,
Have you no youthful secret to tell us?
To us, the sons of sons of your lovers of glory?

Telling us of the shadow too, and of the dream (twin
Weavers of a veil illuminating your nudity),
And telling us, with a laugh, of a rhythm that would be
Your victorious gait!

Not that we should weep, weary of waiting;
Not that we should blaspheme your joy in our sadness:
For here we are, gathering the twigs of your willows
To seek on the flute, in the greening grass,
The shiver of its quaking leaf
For having grazed your shoulders with a kiss...

Helen, we shall sing this evening,
And hour after hour, and until your stars appear,
And well into the night, and until living
In harmony with your soul, and until seeing
Your chaste veils shiver with delight,
Whose secret is revealed;

Helen, we shall sing this evening.

First Song

Doubtless,
The song of chaffinches,
From copse to copse, told the road
Where we passed
From song to song,
My dreams and I, guided
According to the Hour and the Age
– Excellent team! –
A double yoke engarlanding their head
And violet-purple embridled,
Which drew our cart toward the sounds of festivity!

And, from rose to laughter
And from flowers to women,
The road was worse
Where we walked
Holding the lyre
My dreams and I, guided
According to the phrase read on wrinkled parchments
– Which leave their wrinkle on souls; –

But from them to you,
From those to You, the only one,
The endless road stretches
Where the wheel is slow and grates like a grindstone.
Where the cart bogs down or scrapes the side;
And if it was not to listen, at the stopping place,
To what a dream recounts,
To gather from the talus what grows there of hope,
What sorrow, what blasphemy, and what deceit
To walk toward a goal that moves and that escapes me!

An adolescent dream, of a look so tender
That its gentle tale seems to sing
–The teller, who is made to repeat, to hear him
Sing what he thought he was telling –
Told this (what his voice alone made clear):

"... I saw her –
It was on the dusty esplanade
Where the elms are grey
And the ground cracks with thirst
In the August shadow;
And all turned green again on her arrival
And the breeze sang in the surprised elms
Like a sudden shower;
And I felt death in my happy heart;
She came to me
– But who could say whence?
And who knows why? –
On the dusty esplanade..."

Here is another – a dream, young and pale,
Pale, and blushing when it spoke,
With a voice older than it looked and male,
In a slow rhythm,
Which, less muted, would have told of triumphal Glory; –

"... On the sand of the shore
Where every step is erased by the sea wind
That rolls its dunes, in broad slow waves,
Toward the dead cities of the future;
She came to me like a bright wave,
Breaking into laughter at the moving sands;
But I understood that her gaze was doing
Merely the work of memory,
That the words she spoke were no longer true;

For hour hastens hour, and dune drives dune,
Over the cities and dead hearts of the future –
By chance of paths, I was one, she was one..."

They speak, I smile
Or weep or dream
And resume the path that stretches toward evening;
The same as yesterday, less weary, I resumed it
In escape from deceit;

Is it not true that you appear to us
Under the finery of this one, or that one?
Are they not yours, their done-up smiles?
And all those tales told
At the stopping place?
Are you not all that,
Helen, with the incomparable eyes
Towards which stretches, over there,
The road where my tireless walking stick taps
Its alert rhythm
Two times less hurried than my footsteps
Sounding on the open road...
The strength of their impression, is that not you?

Ah! the pain of my joy, scattered and caught off guard:
I have a fear of memories, perfumes, music,
Old cities and autumn orchards,
And the laughter that passes and the hour that strikes,
For everything is unknown, sublime, and without reply;

Thus, the sun lived in its slightest ray,
And what grass dreamt of its blazing glories?
And who would divine in the tears of the dew
The vast sea swelling as far as the septentrion?

Thus the immense plain, widening our dreams,
Suscitates the Infinite only to lose itself in emptiness,

Thus the mad ecstasy with its brief splendors –
They dazzle our eyes to the point of blindness:
I fear all joy in its sad mystery,
Even a futile love moves majestically,
So that all my heart objects and resists
And weeps uncontrollably before your attested dream!

> The pain, Helen, this evening is sweet,
> Among your willows, appear to us.

Second Song

Cadent a latere tuo mille et decem millia a dextris tuis. – Ps. 90[2]

O tall gentle ash trees that smile
– For many a year – not a soul in the wood
Has come to gather the laurels;
And, for many a year, not a soul
– O meadow, at the ford! – has harvested you;
For many and many and many a year
Life has given itself to a beautiful Death
In the young embrace of renewal,
So that Atropos, astonished, hesitates,
Before cutting the thread.

Who then must gather the laurels?...
No vine-shoot yet in the vineyards.
Barely any leaves on the mulberries
(Ah! all the noble desires
That smiled on us);
The lilacs, already sad! and the asphodels;
The hyacinths and the mellowness of the evenings in them;
The white almond trees, hastily adorned;
The apple trees where autumn's hope bursts forth;
The jonquils – here are their sprays –

---

[2]*Cadent...*: Latin for "A thousand shall fall at thy side, and ten thousand at thy right hand..." Psalms 91:7, (KJV).

And the young million of grasses,
Audacious and jovial
Like a bunch of children,
Swell at the tocsin of Prairial:
Enthusiasm, superb choir,
Old Future, blooming again, triumphant!

April wept, smiling through its tears;
Our pride – it was to live,
Seeing ourselves in the unconscious pride of the flowers;
O youth of the World,
Our pride – yours! – was to survive
We, the youngest shoots of the fecund trunk.
Since then (O vanity!):
The deep sleep of hearts beneath the aureoled dawn
Startled us with a shiver
And the world appeared a vast mausoleum
Where humanity lies
Teeming with base desires
Over which, vain souls, we pass
With our calls for help, useless volley,
From over here, to over there.

And since then:
The year has died many times,
In Autumn, in the woods,
And, many times, has been reborn, smiling,
And the Apriline weather that laughs and weeps
And sings
That Time is an illusion;

These have gone, those are dead;
We understood the solitude
Subtle in its remorse;
We almost divined the secret of its silence
Wherein the soul bares itself
And surges beyond sordid words

In its beauty,
Like a beggar woman
To the sculptor she guides
In her serene nudity.

But, one by one,
– Like leaves in autumn –
The desires and dreams fell withered,
Without verdure, without fragrance
– Debris from the crown –
All dead, that no pity pardoned;
But their edified knowledge
Said: this is false, that is vain;
So much so
That with Life, thus denied,
Nothing remained but the desire to live better,
Nothing but the hope that nothing kills,
Nothing but hatred and pious contempt,
Nothing but blind faith that struggles on.

For see, Helen,
These, your priests, flushed with shame,
These who wanted you vain
According to their senile, childlike soul,
These whose too-sad orgy usurps
The tiara of your imperious cult,
Their soul is vile
Beneath expansive skies!

Helen, invoked on my knees,
Appear to us! between the willows.

Third Song

But if a man walk in the night, he stumbleth, because there is no light in him. – JOHN 11:10.

In the ornate choirs of cathedrals
Stretch, like shadows on flagstones,
In rows nearly effaced beneath the footsteps,
Those of old, lords and ladies,
With their devices engraved;

In the ornate choirs of cathedrals,
One still sings
– Though all dreams have been consummated; –
I gazed toward the ogival and sonorous shadow
Where, one by one, the flames die,
As if, forever, over there,
To the less sonorous sounds of the cortege,
Our souls were being carried away.

In the ornate choirs of cathedrals,
Beneath the stained glass of pale smiles,
One still sings the hymn that makes my heart bleed
To love and die and be reborn...
Was there ever a time when, seeking who might embrace you,
Pain, appearing to the mournful soul,
You came, opening your arms, as if to shelter,
And made it smile at its shame adorned
With an abject diadem from which its brow yet! bleeds?

Vexilla Regis...³ obsequies!
To bear the standard, not one man remains even:
Scarcely one head is bowed before the specter...
The majestic Word from abyssal depths,

---

³*Vexilla Regis*: Latin for "Banners of the King." It is also the incipit of a hymn written by Venantius Fortunantus, the Merovingian Bishop of Poitiers.

The desperate Word with echoes of Solyme[4]
Rises in blue incense toward the green-gold stained glass,
Rhythmed by the voices of Rome,
Queen of battle!

Misunderstood Word, but such that, in your shadow,
The sin of knowledge falters before embraces of the Faith:
A voice where the tender sorrow puts even dread to sleep,
Vain voice, and false voice, even a dead voice within me...
O obsequies!

Before, weary, one grew accustomed
To smiling at oneself before the accursed hour,
I looked into my troubled soul:
What hymn would retell the love that burns and slays,
The evening prayer on my trembling lips,
And my exultant joy, fully dressed in flames,
And all the pain of its crushing desire...
Its lassitude, which madly strives,
Renounced the effort, one evening, and seemed to me
So vain that I opened my eyes before your blue veil,
Night, when I smiled like a child that is called,
And when, turning toward the eternal aurora,
I quietly prayed, Childhood, to your star.

The quiet celebration!
And the return, and the lull;
My peace was to sing your dream,
Soul of childhood, virgin of sad prayer;
For all this, ever since poems have been sung,
Is the voice, in an echo, of a single moment of Life
That wells up, finally! and that persists;
My peace was to sing your dream
And, returned from the shadow where all roads end,
I saw your evangelical star
Speaking aloud the words you dreamt in silence,

---

[4]*Solyme*: old name for Jerusalem.

Childhood, it was your voice, this music:

To have been on the parterre of Life,
For one passive hour of immeasurable joy,
That with which the earth adorns itself;
To have lived the satisfied hour
Under the glory of the azured firmament;
To have been for one instant of the mystery;
In the concert of marvelous life
To have been some hovering note,
And to speak it in an echo over the maddening life...

Since yesterday, see, I walk alone and solemn,
In step with the new choice of my ancient hopes
Which would like to live, finally, to be reborn, and to live again;
Evening! envelope us in your grave mystery;
I am cold in soul, hungry in heart, and my spirit is drunk
On all that one hears at the great crossroads.

I shall walk more certain of the goal and of the way
In the intuitive shadow where all roads are effaced
And, closing my eyes, I am dazzled with the joy
Of contemplating the splendor of your face with all my heart,

Helen,
Helen, with the serene lips,
Helen, with your red hair,
Amidst your willows, appear to us.

Fourth Song

> *... For us, it's a blinding of lightning, then a long darkness, – then another lightning.* – R. W. EMERSON

A fleeting shadow exists at each bend of the road;
One smiles from orchard to the trellises of the hedge;
A modesty melts among the rose garden;

Someone sings who falls silent for whoever listens:
And one speaks very quietly near the source that drips:
The day is smiling with faery doubt,
And it is Life – o my heart – all of it;

Also, for fear of a deception,
For fear, also, of missing the alone hour
One lives (is this living?) amorous and mocking,
Joyful and sad, hopeful in despair,
For better or for worse
– According to the law that makes the morning and the evening,
The shadow and the light,
And the winter and the spring which is verdurous,
The law of every love,
Of every joy.

In this way one sings this phrase:

"Drink from the cup of ecstasy
And drink the bitter wine;
All the bitterness of the sea
Is sweeter than that wine that the fatal night
Crushed in its stride;
For its lees are the salt of tears,
And shame sees its pale reflection in it,
And impure death has grown drunk on it..."

Or again according to the hour and the flesh:

"Drink from the cup of ecstasy
And drink the clear sweet wine
– So sweet that the vast ocean would be sweetened by it;
Here is the wine that the joyful night
Crushes in its wine press;
The tears are sweet in its yellowing shade
And the modesty swoons, feeling faint,
And Life is drunk on hope..."

Some other evening, one sings within oneself:

"Listen in the shadows near you:
A sob dies and all is quiet;
What dream have you come to kill?
Take then and drink the sad poison
Without a remorse resisting inside you
Without a regret persisting inside you,
What dream have you come to kill?..."

Then, the rhymes redouble until one is intoxicated by them:

"Listen in the shadows near you:
A laugh bursts out that a kiss drinks in;
What dream will be eternalized?
Take then and drink the joyful wine,
So that pride is affirmed and believes
And so that hope spreads over you;
What dream will be eternalized?..."

In this way I sing and live, and will live, until evening,
O beautiful Helen, hidden in your willows,
Sad and joyous with the same thought,
In the incredulous expectation of seeing you;
Our song is insane,
Helen, and our old hearts are crazy,
You, sole worshipped goddess,
Among your willows, hear us, bowing,
Helen, Helen, appear to us.

Fifth Song

Here is my thought:
If the arrow
That my bow launches at the stars
Drops back down and wounds
The hand that launched it
At the stars;
And if opprobrium
That I cry out to the echo of the woods
– Long-winded or in sober response,
According to my voice –
Returns like an insult
That burns the heart within me;
In this way, a very old dream with respect to you,
A very old emotion
(That a new laugh, it believes, achieves)
Surges again like a tumult,
Helen,
And a very old dream
Weighs on me, night and day, in purposeless shame
Like a remorse:
Such is the hope of a dawn that never rises,
So that my day is weary of bearing my dead days!

I have driven my chase into the heart of the forest,
Nevertheless;
No ripple on the surface of the pond where Diana was surprised;
And I have sought, meanwhile, the dryad promised
Amidst the old oaks like the singing voice
Of someone whose name of glory is laureate.
No lost nymph in the detours of the coppices
Through the deserted path that I cut toward the forest's edge,
After my shameful chase;

But always your desire and your shadow in the ferns

And the voice among voices, whispering, light,
Always a gay desire of adorned verdure,
As on the April morning when I broke my arrows
Knowing (you told me about it in a clear, fresh kiss)
That it is you who wept for the gentle deer brought low...

The path I cut through the woods,
Through the coppices, under the trees,
Has led me to your meadow
And the songs borne
On the evening wind
Resonated as far as the wood;
Like those that I have sung your praise with,
Seeing that they prayed to you under the slow, clear night
Helen,
Listen, in your willows and in your waves,
O beautiful sovereign.
Through me, the sound of the horn makes its way through the vales
From ash to oak
And from hornbeam to birch.

Those men whose face I do not know
Gave their voice to my thought:
And if I repeated it in my own language
It happens that they did not know all my thought:
They did not know how the matinal footpaths,
Through the ferns or over the felt of pines,
Led – like the road with equal ruts
Or the trail worn by passing footsteps,
Like all paths –
Toward your meadow where joy in a thousand floras pierces
The old charnel ground of former springtimes;

But here I am with them, saying, in the gentle words
Of their songs borne

On the vesperal breeze
From prairie
To wood,
Escorted with perfumes:
Helen, come, this evening is gentle,
Among your willows, appear to us.

Last Song

Incerta et occulta sapientiæ tuæ manifestati mihi – PSALMS 51.

O night in full bloom!
Arms wide open toward your deifying embrace,
I wept to be alone to love you in silence;

O night! my soul trembles;
May a soul come and we will pray together;
One weeps to be alone to love you in silence...

And that is why, for days, months, and years
I walked singing in the crowds, [who were] led
By every poor illusion, impure with vile desires,
Begging some echo for my dreams of April.

And that is why, among the babbles of springtime,
On the lookout for new hearts and young moments,
I have said, like others, that it is sweet
To live and pray for the Lover with the red hair
Whose aureole is like radiant flesh;
And that is why I have spoken, at the early hour sounded,
Of the sweetness of going, together, through a childhood orchard;
To feel beating in me the hearts of those who love,
And so that a small part of my poems might live in them;
For one weeps, thus alone to love you in silence.

But you know that I know all vain phrases,
That your silence is the only superhuman voice
And the only brightness, your star-filled darkness,
When one hears the angels passing, in upward flight...

Come, dear, you are the gaiety of all smiles,
You, the sweet justice of Life,
You, the panacea,
You, the ray or reflection of all Thought,
Shadow of young Love – following it, or followed –
The things one says are futile, or worse;

You, you know the Secret, forbidden even to lyres:
The night is upon us in its ineffable joy;
Our kisses and the echo of poems – glory!...
– The glory, that no one attains – are not worth the victory
Of dominating its dream and silencing it forever...
Helen, o Evoked One in unnamed rhythms,
From among the gray willows, appear, proud Queen,
For see how the Prayer grows silent.

Helen

Here I am;
I have been here since yesterday, and since the day before it,
Elsewhere, here;
All flesh, one evening, adorned my old soul
Like the eternity of desire that you don.
The night is bright in the firmament...
Look with your eyes lifted:
Behold – like a tissue of pale, fatal fire
That makes the flower bloom in order to make it wither –
My veil, where all appeasement shows through,
Which calls you to life and which makes you die for it.

The night is bright in the vital firmament...

My myths, you know them:
I am the daughter of the Swan,
I am the moon that makes the oceans exuberant,
That rise, fall, heave again;
And it is the flow of Life, exultant and prostrate,
The flow of dreams,
The flow of flesh,
The vast swell's flux and reflux.

My doubt – one calls it Hope – makes distinguished action:
I am the queen of Sparta and that of Troy,
Through me grievous existence wages war,
I dissolve all inertia in the illusions of my joy,
Helen, Selene, floating from phase to phase,
I am the inaccessible and the third Hypostasis
And if I threw back, as I desire,
My veil which promises, but refuses, ecstasy,
My fiery nakedness would resorb Lives...

FIN

Envoi

All the illusion of Life is in your prodigious hands,
All my poor treasure pales beneath your step;
But the Hour is unmoving, and Art is tireless
If I lift my eyes and look at your dear, lilac eyes;

The shadow that proceeds or follows you according to the hour
Is so frail at your feet that one does not think, on seeing it,
That without you, sweet joy, and without me whom it grazes,
It will depart from here on earth, your final evening;

The morning is gentle, and here You are; look,
Seize the Hour in your gentle eyes to shine it back at me
– Does anyone know what solemn strophe memory keeps?
And does anyone know the hour when death may pardon?

Appendix

The following text is from chapter one, book two, of *Francis Vielé-Griffin: His Work, His Thought, His Art* by Jean de Cours.

Francis Vielé-Griffin: His Thought

Introduction: Positive Values

It seems to me that after having cast a rapid glance over the work of a poet, if one desires to understand him better and know him more intimately, it is of course his thought that we must focus our attention on, and before his thought we must pause a moment even. A poet's thought is the very matter of his poems. Doubtless, it does not constitute his entire work, but it makes up the entire interior part of it, which is as essential as the other; it characterizes the quality of his soul and also the quality of that beauty that art will then render sensible. It is in such a state of mind that we approach the study of Francis Vielé-Griffin's thought.

I would like to set aside from the very start the objection that could be addressed to me, by affirming that a work of art has no other end than its proper beauty, that the poet is not at all expected to think, and that it is pointless, or pedantic, to scan the images that he offers us for a guiding idea that he himself perhaps was not aware of. I know that there is, in favor of this reproach, the distinguished example of Renouvier, looking for and finding in Victor Hugo's work an entire philosophy that Hugo himself would have been very incapable of putting there. However, and whatever one may say, this philosophy did in fact exist. There would have been quite a few others, contradictory amongst themselves, to such a point that we can affirm that those ideas, daughters of the metaphorical or verbal genius of the poet, were found to be quite latent in Victor Hugo's work, if not completely unconscious; also, the Romantic poet himself was mistaken to take himself for a thinker. The role infinitely exceeded the esthetic that his school claimed to realize.

The argument is of little worth if one becomes attached to the work of a symbolist poet, the symbolism striving to be *the reintegration of the idea in poetry*: "all symbolism," wrote Brunetière, "supposing an idea without whose support it is nothing more than a tale told by a nanny; and every symbolic system implies or requires, to be perfectly honest, a metaphysic, by which I mean a certain conception of man's relationship with ambient nature, or, if you prefer, with the unknowable."

This is the point of view then that we must adopt when examining the work of F. Vielé-Griffin, the symbolist poet *par excellence*. And we will thus discover, beneath the symbols, images, dramas, or legends, a thought so simple, so unary, and so logical that that very simplicity, unity, and logic will serve for us as a guarantee that we have not been mistaken; that thought, we will study it in itself, for itself, in its manifestations. We will see it extricate itself from that "vision" to which all the feelings of youth run, as do the stronger, more serious ideas of a mature age, while traversing the hours of crisis whose trouble attests to us its sincerity, to finish finally at a veritable philosophy, not at all abstract, but concrete, very much alive, lived even, in which each poem will be a moment.

Believing, with M. H. Bergson, that one measures the scope of a philosophical doctrine "by the truth of the ideas wherein it flourishes and by the simplicity of the principle wherein it gathers," we will admire that the thought of the poet is inextricably connected to the evolution of his ideal of life and, at the moment of situating it in the large current of contemporary ideas, we will dare to declare it infinitely original, fecund, consoling, and beautiful.

Chapter One [Book Two]

Thought and Poetry

Having defined in some sort the thought of the poet as a constant collaboration between his personality and life, the matter also his poem; [then,] to study the thought of the poet is to study his inspiration. We can, it seems to me, and less arbitrarily than one thinks, distinguish in M. F. Vielé-Griffin three moments. The first, which extends from his beginnings to about the year 1898, the epoch in which *La Partenza* was composed. During this period, the poet sings his feelings, his joy, and conceives little by little his idea of Life, which will become something like the central radiating point of his thought. *La Partenza* marks a second period, a kind of drama or knot in the evolution of the poet's ideal. From the composition of the *Légende ailée de Wieland le Forgeron*, which appeared in 1899, begins a third period during which the poet, with *Amour Sacré*, the *Légende de Bellérophon Hippalide,* and the entire collection of *Voix d'Ionie*, the most recent collection, will offer us the response and the solution to the agonizing problem that his intelligence and heart had posed themselves

During the entire first stage of F. Vielé-Griffin's thought, let us try to discover and note, in the very light of his poems, the feelings from which the ideas are born, the play of principal ideas between them, and their effect in turn on his feelings: let us attempt in sum to evoke the psychological life of the poet. We would be at a loss, in the beginning, to know how to ask of a young man that he offer us a system of coherent and logical, profound and new, ideas: but how new already F. Vielé-Griffin's sensibility proved to be, and how fine already were the views that his intelligence proposed to us.[5]

---

[5]Original footnote: Among the critics who are preoccupied with F. Vielé-Griffin's work, two principally have become attached to his thought. Monsieur Tancrède de Visan consecrates his first chapter of *The Attitude of Contemporary Lyricism* to F. Vielé-Griffin and his idea of Life. I point out the great interest of that study as well as the interest of the study that M. Robert de Souza published on F. Vielé-Griffin's

The Feeling for Nature

From the beginning, that which revealed an entirely original poetic temperament in F. Vielé-Griffin was, in addition to his so personal form, his feeling for nature. It seemed truly like a "breath of fresh air" that penetrated, with him, our literature. That feeling for nature is delicious; so natural, sincere, spontaneous, and exact is it. With it, in fact, we perceive landscapes, appreciated as they are, for what they are, without any concern for the produced effect. No more torrents among apocalyptic rocks, no more lakes necessarily mirroring a horizon of mountains. The light of the moon will, from now on, do without the cemeteries, gothic vaults, and cypresses.

The ordinary, the familiar, replaces the exceptional. The rare no longer draws attention. Any aspect whatsoever of nature charms, retains, exalts F. Vielé-Griffin. His inspiration knows how to draw its strength from any corner whatsoever of the landscape of France, that which one meets with every day, on exiting the city. He will confide to us, one day, that everything moves him, doubtless because he knows how to find some sympathy and some beauty in all things.

The poet has enough tears for the lot of us.[6]

Yes, of course; but he does not stop particularly at any sorrow; and, before the emotion that fills him when standing before nature, if happy in its universality, he despairs almost to be able to translate it.

O, has there ever been in other Aprils
A similar feast under the branches?
And how vain is the palette![7]

---

poetry (*Grande Revue*, Jan 25, 1914). He synthesizes the poet's thought in that simple definition of "l'Amour et la Mort." I will remark in passing what I owe to both the one and the other of these studies, and also in what way my feelings differ from them, but the reader, desirous of an ever necessary supplement of information, must refer to them directly.

[6]The poet's has...: from the poem "May Flower," *Joys*.

[7]O, was there ever...: from the poem "Euphonies," *Cull of April*.

And M. Robert de Souza perfectly expresses in what way a like feeling for nature differs from the analogous, harmonized feelings by Hugo, Theuriet, Lamartine, Verlaine, Paul Fort, who remain city-dwelling folk, and even Francis Jammes, although he takes pleasure remaining a country person. For it is not only Nature that F. Vielé-Griffin confesses a sensibility for, it is primarily the charms of the countryside; and Touraine has become his province of choice. He lived there, in those days, at Nazelles, near Amboise, and, after having abandoned it for several years, he could not resign himself however to quit it completely, given he has returned and established himself there again, not far away, on the other side of the Loire, in La Thomasserie. No poet, unless it is Ronsard or du Bellay, has depicted and loved Touraine as Francis Vielé-Griffin has. And if, in his first poems, he sang of the sea, which revived in him obscure Gaelic sympathies, it is subsequently the river and the plain that get so involved in his inspiration, that a memory of any sort will reawaken their memory. And I believe that he is really standing before the scene evoked by that stanza, under Tourainian skies, which are so soft and blue, walled in by the hills that have such pure lines, when F. Vielé-Griffin felt in his heart his ideal of Life define itself:

> *Already, for our astounded gazes, the plains*
> *Lie in matutinal splendor and joy,*
> *Under the tender sky that a pale haze drowns*
> *In its dream; and around us a sound of breaths,*
> *Rises among the branches and the horizon outspreads*
> *The vaporous immensity of the distant plains.*

And this feeling for nature is so profound, so spontaneous, in the poet that, even after a new lesson in beauty from Greek art will have been sought, neither a countryside that is a bit rude, nor a light that is almost too bright, will have dried up in him the divine power of enjoying and feeling to the point of recreating it, no matter what aspect of nature it might be. Francis Vielé-Griffin, over time, will never lose his freshness of impression; his sensibility when faced with the external world will remain absolutely the same. Neither naïvety, nor the verity of youth, nor the simplicity of his emotion will wither. Let's open, in order to convince ourselves of it, the last collection of the poet to date, *Voix d'Ionie*, and let's read from the

purely lyrical part of the beginning of say "Vision de Midi" or "Qua-
tres Chansons françaises." We will find intact, and deeper perhaps,
that feeling for nature, which had burst out in as early as *Cull of
April*, in order to harmonize more perfectly still in *Clarté de Vie*.

> *Voice of Life, I am as if drunk to hear you:*
> *you are grave in the radiant silence*
> *like the voice of those who smile and who know,*
> *like the quavering accent of avowals, of adieux...*
> *and you place your hands lightly over my eyes,*
> *Fine summer's light.*

By a sort of miracle, the poet has remained the same. Even
though his thought finds pleasure contemplating serious and grave
subjects, it sometimes makes a detour to follow down this road:

> *Matinal, she escapes*
> *The blue kiss of the forest:*
> *That which crosses her hurtles*
> *Down, laughs at the river, and vanishes.*
> *To catch her at a cross breeze,*
> *One would go into the sky perhaps?*
> *By the door of azure that iridesces*
> *The dawn of eternal summits...*

And it will always tarry to listen to "the tall pines where the
breeze is plaintive," in the evening, "where the millstones are warm"
in order to continue seeking "the exhilarating breeze and the mad-
ness of haymaking."

The Image of the World

Thus, F. Vielé-Griffin, from his beginnings in literature as with all
his work, affirms himself to be a poet enamored with the natural
world and simplicity, a poet for whom the exterior world exists. He
will continue to treat sensitive things less as "real illusions" than as
illusions to be verified. The world, such as it is, remains incomplete,

and it is in ourselves, in our impressions, and in our feelings that it is to be realized in some sort. From there, a perpetual and constant concern to harmonize nature with his own heart. It was in his idealism even that he attained a veritable realism, verifying thus a quite fine view held by M. Henri Bergson, who affirms that it is only when "idealism is in the soul that realism shows in one's work." That work was, with F. Vielé-Griffin, the simple game of his intelligence. In 1891, responding to the survey by Jules Huret, Henri de Régnier declared his soul to be "one of the most complete intelligences of this time," and the remark is meant in all senses, only if we recall that in the same survey Maurice Barrès ironically discovered that, even in art, the poet was not, as certain critics seem to believe, "a slave to reality."[8] From the first moment, intelligence organized and prolonged the very fresh data of sensibility and led F. Vielé-Griffin to note correspondences, already suggested by Baudelaire, the which are like the very soul of poetry, divulging themselves across the universe. Thus, realizing the very goal of art, F. Vielé-Griffin, as a true lyrical poet, completes nature by all the riches of his own temperament. A strophe from the distant *Cull of April* makes us understand in what meditation the landscape is completed:

> *The conscious dream that gives you my life*
> *Is sad with the regret of future abandonments,*
> *And the merry path, where age invites us*
> *For one hour's stopover where we linger*
> *In this joyous dream that gives you my life,*
> *Leads us to the next crossroads of abandonments...*
> *O the merry path where love invites us*
> *And the languid stopover where we linger!...*

And always in the same sense, F. Vielé-Griffin will write this strophe, from *Joys*:

> *The grass is taller, in this way, for my bent head,*
> *Than the hills turning blue in the distance;*
> *And everything in life is similar, isn't it,*
> *Foolish soul attached to your shadow,*
> *O you who follow yourself step by step,*

---

[8]Original footnote: Henri Clouard. Response to the inquiry by Émile Henriot.

Bent over yourself,
Life is like that, isn't it?

A similar interpretation of the world shows itself more and more developed, more and more perfect, more and more total, throughout his entire work. We will see it animate the gentlest of *Chansons à l'Ombre*, and blossom in *Vision de Midi*, where nature is incorporated into universal life to the point of appearing to the poet like the ancient crown weaver herself. His intelligence, after his sensibility, is bound by fate to lead F. Vielé-Griffin to Symbolism.

The Flower of Joy

But this so vivid feeling for nature, this being taken possession of by the external world, would not know how to isolate itself, in reality, from other feelings felt or sung by the poet. One must admire in each poem how they blossom into beautiful and noble ideas, which are so coherent, so logical, and so human that their own worth, even more than the intention of the poet, raises them to the rank of a veritable philosophy.

The feeling that F. Vielé-Griffin was pleased to exalt above all other feelings is joy; and Remy de Gourmont has already pointed it out in his *Book of Masques*: "I do not wish to say," he wrote, "that F. Vielé-Griffin is a joyful poet, however he is a poet of Joy. With him, one participates in the pleasures of a normal and simple life, with the desire for peace, with the certitude of beauty, with the invincible youthfulness of nature. He is not violent, nor sumptuous, nor gentle: he is calm. Although very subjective, or even because of it, for to think of oneself is to think completely of oneself – he is religious." Before he gave the title *Joys* to his collection of poems of 1889, he expressed himself like this on many pages in *Cull of April*:

Here is, for the span of one hour, a riverine dream.
The sands and the grey willows, and the serene
Expanse of clear sky, and all the prairies
To the west where heifers graze

On flowers and sweet grass; and thus may you live,
Ignorant of whatever chance has led you here,
O laugher of the unconscious laugh, dreamer of the
Merry dream of April forests where a song of sap surges.

For the day is joyous and the river falls asleep...

And F. Vielé-Griffin will speak to us so frequently of his joy, that he deserves to be called the poet of Joy, as well as the poet of Touraine or the poet of Life. One must above all see in his joy the expression of a fine mental health. A man harmoniously balanced cannot, in F. Vielé-Griffin's thought, stifle his proper joy when faced with the great scenes of nature.

O radiant gardens that birthed me!
And I see each hour and all your seasons again:
Joy, in the laughter of bright leaves by the strand,
Joy, in the lake-blue smiles on the horizons,
Joy, in the prostrations of the passive plain,
Joy blossoming in shivers;
The youthful delights that were in our eyes,
– Auroras and sunsets – the stars in the skies,
And the portal of life, open and spacious,
Around the time of young harvests!

And Griffin will sing that joy, on almost every page of his work. But we would be mistaken if we confused the joy of the poet with a simple intoxication of the senses, or with a sort of pantheistic exaltation, which we find again, adorned with magnificent accents, in Madame de Noailles or Paul Fort. Doubtless, there is a bit of that in the joy of F. Vielé-Griffin, but there is primarily something else. The joy can come from an intoxication of the senses, but it comes above all from the heart. A veritable heart feels joy emanating from every activity, each time it has made an effort in the direction of beauty, love, or simply life. And F. Vielé-Griffin's joy is not even a joy without reason, a Romantic joy, it is a conscious, well thought-out and deliberate joy. Let us not take that joy, either, for the sign of a fundamental and beatific optimism, for the sign of an incapacity of the poet to feel, to experience, to express a complete series of human feelings, which include grief, sadness, regret. Those feelings, F. Vielé-Griffin experiences them all as intensely as the Romantic poets, and we would find, over the course of his poems, innumerable expressions of them:

The roses along the way evoke other roses;

So that, in the evening that arrives, my soul is sad
Vaguely, without regret, if it isn't with a hope
And that my gentle and impetuous heart might resist
With the promises of a loving shadow and, in the evening
That comes very slowly over us, my soul is sad.[9]

Elsewhere he writes:

Let my love drift far away on the ocean
And by your voice cradle its dream asleep;
For tomorrow, it must weep for all this emptiness.[10]

In the middle of his poems of *Joys*, he will note this impression of infinite and grievous sadness:

Not even the echo of young laughter anymore,
– Some lizards fall like flakes from the walls –
And no reflection of her smile
But in the flowers whose smiles jest;
Dead hours hang motionless on the sill;
It feels like someone is opening a coffin.

But a strophe from "The Stopping Place," in the collection *Swans*, better than any commentaries can do, will reveal to us the meaning that the poet discovers in both his joy and his sadness. He seems to have summarized his entire future thought therein, and to have had a prophetic intuition of the trouble that will invade him one day, and which he will be forced, so frankly and so courageously, to triumph over. We are be unable to be surprised by it, given that the poet spends his life making clear to himself what he feels most inter-

[9]The roses... is sad: from "Mystical Hour," *Cull of April.*

[10]Let... emptiness: from "Euphonies," *Cull of April.*

nal, and as if most hidden:

> *O! Believe me! [You] who think on the morrow:*
> *Excessive joy is sorrowful and so much so*
> *That the soul, in its grief, exults immortal,*
> *To weep is sweet above all else;*
> *Sit down beside me;*
> *When I wept, head in hand,*
> *I saw, between my fingers, that slow grey light turn pink:*
> *At that time, my soul had faith.*
> . . . .
> *Sit down, my sister, and weep:*
> *To weep is beautiful above all else;*
> *It is only one hour, but it lasts*
> *Eternal in metamorphoses:*
> *The hour of holy pity and superhuman love*
> *That weeps until it smiles... at last.*

F. Vielé-Griffin is too complete a poet not to seize, in the hour that passes, the least of its aspects. He feels himself overcome by the sadness, but he refuses to stop, to analyze that feeling that he judges not very human, by which I mean not very worthy of a man. It is in the direction of joy that he wants to go. Perhaps he thinks, with Spinoza, that it is the way to a greater perfection; perhaps he considers it a state of the soul, without which one does not know how to undertake an ascension toward any goal whatsoever, which a man, and above all the poet, can and must propose to himself. Perhaps it is already the necessary atmosphere for that aspiration towards which he is moving. He knows it is easy and difficult at one and the same time, near and distant, both altogether, around us and primarily within us. Whatever the case... it is joy that he sings:

> *But the Flower of Forbidden Joy is supreme,*
>
> *And it is about this that these poems speak.* [11]

---

[11] But the flower...: from the introductory poem to *Swans.*

His Art

One should not conclude, however, that F. Vielé-Griffin never lets himself be dominated by his feelings. [But] we would be mistaken to take him for a sentimental poet. The most sensitive of poets coexists in him alongside an idealistic poet, by which I mean a poet who can contemplate the beautiful and pure ideas that are born in his mind and people it in harmonious rounds; with F. Vielé-Griffin, ideas are always new, original, and human.

They are also alive, every one of them loaded with memories, colors, experience, I will say. For, if he is idealistic, F. Vielé-Griffin is in no way an intellectualist. He despises concepts when they are dry, and that is clear in all his very first poems, while ideas of art, love, and beauty lead him imperceptibly to that idea of life that will become in its turn the central and radiating point of his entire thought, the basis of all his esthetic, and also of all his moral doctrine... for the poet will refuse one day to distinguish between them.

In many poems of *Cull of April*, F. Vielé-Griffin allows us to hear the conception that he has already formed of art. In speaking to us in animating rhythms, he demonstrates to us that he knows his art, a master making demands on his faithful, not admitting division. Also, in "Dea" he writes:

Imperious Poesy is my lover

And a little later, in the middle of his poems on the sea:

And, like Parsifal in the erotic garden
Among the flowers of evil and their temptations,
I did not dream, that evening, but on the authentic
*   Masterwork*
Where all our passions must converge.

We understand, by such signs, at what height the poet placed his art. His profoundly individualistic tendencies had pushed him to reject, from the beginning, the somewhat superficial and false conception of Parnassian art. Several years after the second half of *Clarté de Vie*, which he will entitle "En Arcadie," the poet will apply

himself to defining his own ideal of art with more rigor. And, en-
lightened by all that we know moreover from the poet himself, cer-
tain poems like "La Coupe" take their *signification* from a veritable
ars poetica. We will have to return to that when we study the poet's
art. For now, very general directions will suffice. Recognizing an
eminently new character in his thought as in his sensibility, F. Vielé-
Griffin has sought, and desired for them, an art that is both particular
and adequate. He refused to confuse art with the profession, that
which is essential with that which is false, that which is natural with
that which one can learn. The Symbolist movement, a profound, vig-
orous, and enthusiastic reaction against the exteriority of Parnassian-
ism and the baseness of Naturalism, while favoring rightly, in that
period, all the tendencies toward individuality, must count F. Vielé-
Griffin among its adepts of the first hour, and soon thereafter among
its leaders. Art, appearing to the poet as the most natural, profound,
and at the same time elevated thing in man, must not, consequently,
be attached to any vain object. Far from being seduced by the then-
reigning theory of art for art's sake, F. Vielé-Griffin will apply him-
self subsequently to demonstrate the non sense implied in a similar
thesis: "Art," he wrote, "is not an entity, not even mental. Art is a
natural function whose end cannot be in itself, any more than masti-
cation or deglutination can be conceived of as being an end in them-
selves... Art is thus a natural function of man, the supreme form of
universal prayer, whose rudimentary form is born from the confused
indices of unconscious life so as to excel at the extreme limit of ge-
nial ecstasy, and the work of art is that perpetuated prayer, by virtue
of the living ex-voto that some very high soul dedicates to Beauty."
We will say then that the formula "art for art's sake" is dead, or it is
transformed into "art for beauty." It is, then, in this idea that F.
Vielé-Griffin has of beauty, that his conception of art is definitively
resolved, just as we shall see this idea of beauty of his resolved and
transformed into an ideal of life.

Beauty

As with his feelings for nature and his desire for joy, so too with his conception of art different than what we can find analogously among the best poets of his time! From his very first verse, the idea of beauty is affirmed by F. Vielé-Griffin as entirely new. Fine and supreme object of art, Beauty appears to the poet as if conserving a small part of that total life which his own research communicates to him. As he had protested against the Parnassian's theory of art for art's sake, and also against the notion of art games, which certain estheticians, disciples of [Gustave] Kant and Schiller, continued to maintain, while waiting for Jean-Marie Guyau to make decisive arguments against them, F. Vielé-Griffin rebels against an entirely exterior conception of Beauty. All that part of the collection of poems entitled "At Helen's Tomb" in *Swans* confides to us, through the transparent veils that the *symbol* dons, the idea of Beauty that the poet creates for himself. Beauty is clearly a happy proportion, a plastic harmony of forms: but it is also more than that. Let us listen to the lament that F. Vielé-Griffin addresses to those loyal to so exterior a Beauty:

> *For see, Helen,*
> *These, your priests, flushed with shame,*
> *These who wanted you vain*
> *According to their senile, childlike soul,*
> *These whose too-sad orgy usurps*
> *The tiara of your imperious cult,*
> *Their soul is vile*
> *Beneath expansive skies!*

Helen, in whom the poet incarnates true Beauty, is something else again, she is much more. She is alternately the face of joy, love, hope: she is, above all, the thousand rays of universal soul like the individual and profound soul:

> *Is it not true that you appear to us*
> *Under the finery of this one, or that one?*
> *Are they not yours, their done-up smiles?*
> *And all those tales told*
> *At the stopping place?*
> *Are you not all that,*
> *Helen, with the incomparable eyes*
> *Towards which stretches, over there,*

The road where my tireless walking stick taps
Its alert rhythm
Two times less hurried than my footsteps
Sounding on the open road...
The strength of their impression, is that not you?

And again:

Come, dear, you are the gaiety of all smiles,
You, the sweet justice of Life,
You, the panacea,
You, the ray or reflection of all Thought,
Shadow of young Love – following it, or followed –
The things one says are futile, or worse;

You, you know the Secret, forbidden even to lyres:
The night is upon us in its ineffable joy;
Our kisses and the echo of poems – glory!...
– The glory, that no one attains – are not worth the victory
Of dominating its dream and silencing it forever...

By despairing of being able to express all the modality, all the richness, of Beauty such as he conceives it, the poet cries out:

And it is Life – o my heart – all of it;

Yes, Beauty really is, for F. Vielé-Griffin, what exists of the profound, fecund, and positive in life, by consequence: it becomes, thus, something intimate and ideal which we can participate in at every hour. When the poet, at the time of *Clarté de Vie*, exalts Beauty again, in [the poem] "Melissa," the symbol will not contradict the symbol of Helen in any way, it will merely accentuate its traits. If Beauty is deployed throughout the universe, in perceptible flowers, in harmonious shapes, let us have no doubt about it, it will have remained the infinitely simple, infinitely sincere and pure fruit of an intensity of life that is entirely interior. We could not, without betraying his conviction, isolate it from whatever it might be, for F. Vielé-Griffin was compelled to write: "Supreme Beauty is total perfection... and the artist does not demean himself nor run from his duty, but persists there to consider, to proclaim to the best of his strength, the just ideal and the true ideal. The artist, by the very fact that he prefers the cult of Beauty, proclaims the Justice of Truth." What results is that art, for F. Vielé-Griffin, is confounded with life, as beauty is confounded with the good. But let us see a voluntary union in this, rather than a confusion. All these ideas are marvelously clear. They are not actually confounded except in the absolute: the men who we are do not grasp anything but modes, as Spinoza said. And that leads us to understand how pursuing any one whatsoever of those ideals completely is equivalent to pursuing all the others. They are given to us altogether, in that supreme kindness, which God confides to us, with the mission of enjoying it fully and increasing it to its extreme limits. That benefit, in F. Vielé-Griffin's thought, is none other than "Life."

Love

But before studying that idea of "Life" in itself, which remains the central point of the poet's thought, it seems to me that we must examine by what particular character his conception of love is nuanced. Nothing is more representative of the temperament of a poet, whoever he may be, than the manner in which he understands and sings love. Nothing, better than the poems by Musset, Lamartine, or Hugo, depicts romantic love for us; nothing, better than the strophes wherein he celebrates his love, will confirm for us what we could already divine of F. Vielé-Griffin's nature.

Well in advance of creating those heroes, Ancaeus, Samia, Swanhilde, Phocas, Wieland, all of whom will encounter love along the way, F. Vielé-Griffin has confided to us, in the very gentle songs of *Cull of April*, *Joys*, and *Swans*, the inspirations that would suggest Love to him.

How simple it was, how frank, how fresh, how natural too, that love! By his tender intimacy, by his supple gaiety, by his contempt for the effect to be produced, by his absence of fatality – how greatly did he stand in opposition to romantic love! To tell the truth, and as M. Robert de Souza very clearly notes, his poetry involves very little of the flesh. It is, with joy, one of the first flowers that life holds out to us, a flower of pure ingenuousness and robust fragrance, wrapped and veiled by a kind of delicious modesty; it is only in depth that he is able to express himself:

> *Your wide eyes, and ingenuous pigtails, and your voice,*
> *Merry and musical, in naïve replies,*
> *And your celestial candor when you explain to me*
> *The fabulous wherefores of the things you see...*

A little later, he will write again, at the end of *Carmen Perpetuum*:

> *Unique hour of thoughtless and chaste love*
> *Burning crepuscule of a radiant summer; –*
> *O the candid and tender Idyll that it was,*
> *Despite the other ill-starred evening that occurred.*
>
> *Seated on your knees in the shade where your shape*
> *Was drowned, I listened to your voice, as if in ecstasy:*
> *Each naïve contour seemed like a phrase to me;*
> *The unexpected and crazy woirds that the spring*
>
> *Breeze brought me from your mischievous lips,*
> *Appeared to ripple around your body:*
> *For me, colors and sounds became confused then*
> *In the intoxication of loving a childlike woman...*

In this way, amorous love, with F. Vielé-Griffin, mixes deeply with his feelings for nature; it is of the same essence, it emerges from the same sensibility, it tends toward the same joy.

Without confounding them, one often meets them mixed together, and they complete each other, spontaneous and frank the two of them. But love, for our poet, is still a principle of exaltation, as these strophes from *Joys* testify:

> *"You, so bright and so golden-blonde and so female,*
> *You, all the dream of springtime nights,*

You, gracious like a flame
And svelte and frail in soul and body,
Gay and light like the banners;
And your smile soaring like a scale
Through the clearings in an echo –"

"You, my pride all proud,
You, the sole goal, sole way, and sole end,
You, by whom alone I dream of being culled,
You, my poem and my thirst and my hunger,
What evening has fallen, what hour has grown old?"

Such is the dialog of lovers. She is fine, gay and golden, laughing, natural; he too is frank and joyful. They express themselves with words that are so simple and so direct, that Verlaine himself, seeking to give himself, in *The Good Song*, a naïve soul, could not find a gentler language by which to welcome and sing his fiancée. And that conception of love will not change in the thought of the poet; however, it might grow deeper and be charged with more possibilities, and also with more significations. Abandoned by Yeldis, after a fantastic ride, the last of the knights will still feel utterly enlightened by the memory of his love:

I have no shame, thinking on it, of myself,
I have not a single regret for that poem:
I know that, to have followed her
Beneath the chestnut trees, I follow life.

Likewise, it will be love, again, that will reveal to Wieland the secrets of his art:

I have broken the work forcibly,
I have conceived of beauty;
I have killed the idea of brutal victory,
I have kissed love,
I have known gaiety...

Through love, behold him now the blacksmith, the goldsmith; and, even abandoned by Alvitte, the regrets that he feels, as searing as they are, never attain that profound me, which love had however so magnificently fecundated. Love will always appear to F. Vielé-Griffin charged with positive riches, with increasing strength. We will never see him attached to those complications and scruples that torment and trouble Baudelaire. He survives himself, and he knows how to grow expansive with each new joy. The reason for this is perhaps that F. Vielé-Griffin never seems to consider it an end in itself, an object to pursue above all others, a passion to appease, as the Romantics wished to. Also, more spontaneous perhaps than in any other poet, so delicate and so juvenile, love, for F. Vielé-Griffin, is always viewed as a vital function, a fruit that life offers as much to the body as to the soul. In this way, he remains submissive to life, he always subordinates himself to that more elevated ideal. Ancaeus, Swanhilde, Phocas will not hesitate, whatever it may cost them, to sacrifice it. One day, however, we will see it considered as the veritable spring of life, and as the end that it must be proposed, as the goal that shines before life and lights it up by its own proper light. But that purified, transfigured love will remain of a different order, and it will no longer be love, but "Sacred Love."

The Idea of Life

It is always the Idea of Life – which we have met with over the course of our analyses – as the principle to that joy, which the poet desired, and which, as a means to that Art, was bound to lead him to Beauty.

It is again to the Idea of Life that the conception of love which the poet made for himself is subordinated. It is the idea of Life that we see everywhere, animating the desires, feelings, aspirations of the Poet to such a degree that we can truly repeat, with M. Tancrède de Visan: "The man of genius, following Hello, is he who has but one idea. Under multiple forms, in the poems of F. Vielé-Griffin, a single thought is found incarnate, the idea of life, or creative activity." That, although a bit brief, is eminently true. Also, it is indeed the idea of life that we find as the nexus or knot of the poet's thought. It is the idea of life that the particular nuances, which we have already examined, participate in, and it is the idea of life that, on another day, will provoke a moment of trouble, an hour of crisis, in F. Vielé-Griffin's life. Big, profound, fecund, and so rich an idea, if one considers that at the time the poet conceived of it the last divagations of the Romantic malady still reigned in literary milieux on the one hand, while the suffocating narrowness of Naturalistic and Parnassian esthetics reigned on the other. An idea so vast that we will be able to point out only some very fragmented aspects of it. In order to define what F. Vielé-Griffin includes under the concept of Life, the luxury of admirable metaphors would be needed, which M. Henri Bergson accumulates over the course of his work, in order to express an analogous intuition. Faced with such complexity, we will return to the always lively source of the poems: and there, pouring over them, we will try to understand how F. Vielé-Griffin felt awakening in himself that idea of Life; then, by successive approximations, we will be compelled to note the characteristics that adorn, one after the other, that idea of Life in the volumes that the poet published in the year 1898 or thereabouts.

I think that it is really in the contemplation of that nature, which inspired a sort of fervor in him, that F. Vielé-Griffin drew the first elements of his idea of Life. Doesn't that idea already seem to animate the strophes of his very first poems and, for example, these several lines of verse from "Euphonies"?

> *Those were sweet hours,*
> *O my lady of blonde roses,*
> *When the swarm of dreams*
> *Whirled in mad rings over the mosses,*
> *And you said sweet things.*

We can find and recognize in it something, nearly unconscious, of the poet's first intuition of Life. Life, it is what reveals to us all nature at first, and then our own heart. It is that mysterious thing still, which will awaken love. Life is that universal force that will reveal to the poet "the surprised wisdom of the radiant mystery of being." Life is what teaches man his own proper existence and his dignity. Addressing himself to a young, twelve-year-old suicide, F. Vielé-Griffin expressed himself thus:

You are a man, they told you sometimes,
And radiant, it was your young pride;
And better it was not to have been born
And to sleep – at large – in your casket.
Better to die as you die, I think,
To turn yourself away from your indignity
. . . .
You were Life swelling in the wind of hope
Of Calvary, in Vendémiaire, drunk on belief;
You were Life in the noisy combats,
And you bravely had yourself killed, before, again,
At the Thermopylae of all your hearths
And, when you died beaming, for the Fatherland!
Of course your heart believed
And of course, in death itself, you were Life.
For Life is beautiful and holy,
Life is joy and sorrow and mystery,
And to die, as you did, fearlessly,
One must love the world's dream.
They lied about it, those who made of it
A crumb of bread, a draught of mortal wine;
They killed you thrice, those who denied
Love and God and your humanity;
But if they made life for you according to their shame,
By rejecting their offered life, you dominate them.

Thus the idea of life soon mixes, in the thought of F. Vielé-Griffin, with the idea of humanity. All those later dramas made that nuance clear. For now, I want merely to point out how life appears to the poet, in the perfectly harmonious synthesis of all living forces, of all exterior and interior forces, of all real as well as all ideal forces. What am I saying? Life is itself an ideal that one must at every instant make an effort to realize, and whose realization already depends on an iron will in each of us:

Believe: Life or Death, what difference to you,
In the glare and dazzle of love?
Pray in your strong soul:

Night or day, what difference to you?

For you will know vast dreams
If you know the one law:
There is no night under the stars
And all shade is within you.

Love: Shame or glory, what difference,
To you, whose turn it is now?
Sing with your voice that carries
The message of all love!
For you will tell the song of splendors
If you tell your intimate emotion:
There are no fatal disasters –
All defeat is in you.

And F. Vielé-Griffin will confide to us, in another delicious song, how, for his own part, he perpetually realizes his idealism:

With a little sun and blond sand
I have made gold,
Whose ardent secret is not cowering
In the vain crucible of athanors:
It fell from my fingers, with the sound
That makes
Flutes gay:
It ran between my fingers
In the moiré water
Of windy games in Messidor.
With dazzling wheat I made the snow
Of old age,
And the pale smile of virgins
Wounded by
A word of strange joy in its promise,
A gesture,
Which dissipates the cortege
Of light dreams whose smile alleges
The march of hours,
– To the sill where love plaits

The empurpled simarre of sacrilege:
I have made snow
With flower petals.

With the hours of hurried and bright life
I have made spiritual eternity:
I have taken a little salt in my hands
And sown it over the bitterness of the sea
In the manner
Of frail things that one dreams eternal
I have taken the salt
Of all our tears, bitter-sweet,
And I have thrown it into death's face.

In the words that F. Vielé-Griffin finds pleasure using to veil his gesture, it is nonetheless easy for us to grasp the meaning of that gesture and to measure its scope. We must not, under pain of grave error, confuse the idealism of the poet with the intellectualism of a Taine for example. When this latter is absorbed in his own analysis, F. Vielé-Griffin's conception leads him from the start to affirm, to exalt the primacy of action over dreams, or rather, to make us hear that, logically, we would be mad to isolate them and separate them from each other. "Action is not the sister of dreams," no, it is something else altogether. At each instant it is action that realizes the dream and makes it participate in all the joys of life. Action completes the dream at every instant, it adds to it all that is possible, all the reality caught glimpse of. Again, it is action by which one is a man, by which he primarily becomes one, by which he proves his own life to himself and others. Thus, through the exercise of Life, a superior sort of humanity is realized little by little. Desire for Life and the will for Life continuously create through themselves a veritable Life, which is a life of desire. Thus, effort discovers its own proper goal. Thus, dreams and action become indissolubly united in this "movement" for which the poet has always confessed to us his pleasure, and by which he rightly defined his symbolism. Thus Life, which is nature itself, also finds itself to be a perpetual creation of the individual. Art becomes the expression of that creation, a new creation essentially arising out of the other and superimposing itself without end. Thus Life, which is dreams and realities, becomes also Joy; for Joy naturally accompanies the exercise of a vital function. Thus life is Beauty, not at all a search for originality or something rare but, according to Charles Maurra's expression, "the splendor it-self of what is normal and familiar." To live, finally, is to participate fully in universal life, in the life each one of us lives, in the life of men born and to be born. And F. Vielé-Griffin will say it to us again and again in the many pages of his work:

> *We live forever in what we love*
> . . . .
> *Nothing dies in us, nothing is futile or vain*
> *The effort that glorifies life is always sane.*

And, similarly, the Poet of the poem "La Coupe," responding to his predecessor the Potter, exclaims, in a sort of prophetic enthusi-asm in the face of that daily "Eternity":

> *Forebear! we are the perpetual voice!*
> *And what lives in us, the ephemerae,*
> *Is eternal in itself, being Life;*
> *Our art is not an art of lines and spheres:*
> *We are, that is enough;*
> *Let us be [one] with all voices:*
> *Tomorrow we will sleep where the silent past sleeps.*
>
> *But the harmonious future will be:*
> *What we were subsists;*
> *So well that on the lips of lovers*
> *The word "Forever" is reborn imperishably,*
> *Joyous and mournful...*

And he expresses, again, where he finds the source of all his riches:

> *What I take from etesian breezes,*
> *Another will take and find himself rich on.*

Yes, F. Vielé-Griffin really thinks that life is eternal, in the sense that Spinoza affirmed, he too, that the soul is, not immortal, but eternal. And not only is life eternal, but it is, as M. Tancrède de Visan remarks, an "eternal return." In many poems, F. Vielé-Griffin evokes before us "the great eternal gesture that turns and rejoins itself," and in "Lumière de Grèce" it is also what the old man Lassos, having become blind, will see in his mind and will confide prophetically to the young Pindar:

> *I see, o my child, o my poet,*
> *The road where everything returns to identity,*
> *Love, hope, glory, beauty;*
> *Child, I see the night of Eternity...*

This here is, then, very certainly, one of the many aspects that adorn, in F. Vielé-Griffin's thought, his idea of life. Does it follow that we must give him the importance that M. Trancrède de Visan attributes to him and, above all, associate with him an analogous idea conceived by Nietzsche in Sils Maria in 1881, which the philosopher expressed in several pages of his *œuvre*? "Man," Nietzsche said, "all his life, like an hourglass, will always be reborn and will forever come back anew... All the states that this World can attain, he has already attained them and not once only, but an infinite number of times." Nietzsche even found pleasure in giving a poetic expression to that idea in his *"Midnight Song,"* written on the balcony of the Villa Barini in Rome, which he himself declared to be the most solitary song ever written:

> *O man! be on your guard:*
> *The world is profound,*
> *And profounder than the day had thought.*
> *Profound is his sorrow;*
> *His joy – profounder still than his suffering.*
> *Sorrow says: Pass and perish!*
> *But every joy wants Eternity,*
> *Wants profound Eternity.*

And we know the consequences of that idea, which could, it seems to me, be summed up completely in a sentence by Kierkegaard, "He who wants the recommencement, he alone is a man."

F . Vielé-Griffin evidently thinks similarly. But that is not his thought's last expression, and that is also not where we must look for the reason for or explanation of the hour of trouble that he will traverse, and which his divine *Partenza* is the sign of. For his own part, F. Vielé-Griffin will look "further." Must we then see, in that encounter between two minds that are so different, an influence or a coincidence? There would not even be a question of influences, the poet frankly avowing not to have known the genial divagations of Nietzsche save on the eve of war and, that, because of a voluntary ignorance perhaps. So we are quite constrained to admit the hypothesis of a coincidence, explained by a parallel research of two intelligences, the one proceeding by an admirably balanced journey, the other proceeding by contradictory bounds and outbursts of genius, but both of them anxious to follow their own way, forgetting all the pre-made formulas and pre-established systems, both thirsty for personal verifications and intimate experiences. The scene of nature, eternally itself and eternally rejuvenated, offered them a point of common departure and the occasion for an identical encounter.

But let us not exaggerate in any way the importance of that coincidence. Let us leave to the idea of the "eternal return" the true place that it occupies in the thought of the poet, and let us subordinate it to that other idea that, above all, Life is eternal. Given this conception of life, what is the attitude that F. Vielé-Griffin will take with respect to it, and what is the attitude also that he will propose to offer us? It can be summed up in a few words: acceptation, to start with, then confidence, and finally love.

Yes, F. Vielé-Griffin accepts and desires that we accept life, such as it is, with its inevitable sadnesses, and the inevitable destructions that its perpetual course brings with it, its eternity. The last words of the *Chevauchée d'Yeldis,* are they not like the cry of wisdom that, joyously, accepts [life]?

> *I followed the furrow that day*
> *And, leaning over the spray that I gathered for you,*
> *I listen to the cowbells in the evening*
> *And think that a life filled with hope is good.*

He has already told us:

Rejoice and learn how to believe.

That confidence, that love, which we must put into life, animates every poem of *Chansons à l'Ombre*. Since the strophes that he placed in exergue, on the sill of *Clarté de Vie*, F. Vielé-Griffin wrote:

Stretch your limbs, life is weary beside you,
– Let it sleep, from morning to evening,
Beautiful, weary,
Let it sleep –
Get up, you: the dream calls you and passes
Into enormous shadows;
And if you delay in believing,
I know not what guide will be there waiting for you
– The dream calls and passes,
In the direction of divinity.

That exaltation of confidence in, and love for, Life colors with a nuance of joyful fervor each inspiration that every passing hour, that every minute of every day, suggests to the poet. Listen to him sing in *Sieste*:

The mystery is illuminated
By slow eternal things,
The dream borders Life,
Souls and flowers blend
And the joyous blood divines
Why the hours are beautiful.

It flows and whirls
From heart to temples, and returns,
Sings, alert and monotonous,
The lullaby of ancient times:
How holy and good life is,
How everything is right and fine...

And again in "Au coin de l'âtre":

Reread, aloud, that tomorrow

We will repay its expectation,
And that the road is always good
For him whose steps make sounds there
And that the source is always new
For the passerby who wets his thirst
And that life is made in this way,
Hazardous and hastily,
Morose, crazy and beautiful,
Perpetual,
So that one lives it.

And finally in "Mai," with the return of spring:

Here, finally, it is sweet to live
Mixed with eternal joy;
The air vibrates with the traits of a drunken violin
That sings between heaven and earth!
I am all that you are,
My thought is your plaything
And your kiss was the poet,
The Singer of God's Orchard!

Although not having yet given, by these citations and by these analyses, anything but a very superficial outline of what F. Vielé-Griffin's idea of Life is, I hope I have not deformed his veritable thought too much. It is easy to see then that there are really a thousand aspects, a thousand nuances to that idea, admirable in their nature and depth, in their fresh and joyous healthiness, which sustain, swell, and exalt his juvenile aspiration. It is really the guiding principle of his work, for that entire period that extends from his beginnings to the year 1897. From that moment forward, we can advance and see how, from that idea, the possibility of an entirely mental drama was given birth to in his thought, which made the poet of Touraine and of Joy a more human poet perhaps, and who will grow closer and closer to all souls.

Other Books by the Publisher

Fanchette's Pretty Little Foot by Restif de La Bretonne

Je M'Accuse... by Léon Bloy

My Hospitals & My Prisons by Paul Verlaine

Salvation Through the Jews by Léon Bloy

Words of a Demolitions Contractor by Léon Bloy

Cellulely by Paul Verlaine

Ecclesiastical Laurels by Jacques Rochette de la Morlière

Flowers of Bitumen by Émile Goudeau

Songs for Her & Odes in Her Honor by Paul Verlaine

On Huysmans' Tomb by Léon Bloy

Ten Years a Bohemian by Émile Goudeau

The Soul of Napoleon by Léon Bloy

Blood of the Poor by Léon Bloy

Joan of Arc and Germany by Léon Bloy

Theresa the Philosopher & The Carmelite Extern Nun by Marquis d'Argens & Anne-Gabriel Meusnier de Querlon

A Platonic Love by Paul Alexis

Two Novellas: Francine Cloarec's Funeral and Benjamin Rozes by Léon Hennique

The Revealer of the Globe: Christopher Columbus & His Future Beatification (Part One) by Léon Bloy

Héloïse Pajadou's Calvary by Lucien Descaves

An Immodest Proposal by Dr. Helmut Schleppend

The Pornographer by Restif de La Bretonne

Style (Theory and History) by Ernest Hello

On the Threshold of the Apocalypse: 1913-1915 by Léon Bloy

She Who Weeps (Our Lady of La Salette) by Léon Bloy

The Sylph by Claude Prosper Jolyot de Crébillon (*fils*)

School of Woman by Nicolas Chorier

Voyage in France by a Frenchman by Paul Verlaine

Ourigan, Oregon by William Clark, Richard Robinson, and anonymous

Drowning by Yu Dafu

Cull of April by Francis Vielé-Griffin

The Misfortune of Monsieur Fraque by Paul Alexis

Fêtes Galantes & Songs Without Words by Paul Verlaine

Joys by Francis Vielé-Griffin

The Son of Louis XVI by Léon Bloy

Septentrion by Jean Raspail

The Resurrection of Villiers de l'Isle-Adam by Léon Bloy

Poems Saturnian by Paul Verlaine

The Biography of Léon Bloy: Memories of a Friend by René Martineau

Fredegund, France: A Book of Poetry by Richard Robinson

The Good Song by Paul Verlaine

www.ingramcontent.com/pod-product-compliance
Lightning Source LLC
Chambersburg PA
CBHW031446120626
46545CB00006B/2582